MW00779077

This Valentine's Day, I Promise You All My Love

This Valentine's Day, I Promise You All My Love

A contemporary collection
of romantic love poems
from Blue Mountain Arts®

Blue Mountain Press ®

Boulder, Colorado

Library of Congress Catalog Card Number: 95-36006
ISBN: 0-88396-421-X

ACKNOWLEDGMENTS appear on page 62.

⌐⌐⌐
|Π| design on book cover is registered in
U.S. Patent and Trademark Office.

Manufactured in the United States of America
First Printing: September, 1995

Library of Congress Cataloging-in-Publication Data

This Valentine's Day, I promise you all my love : a contemporary
    collection of romantic love poems from Blue Mountain Arts.
        p.   cm.
    ISBN 0-88396-421-X (hardcover : alk. paper)
    1. Love poetry, American. 2. Valentine's Day—Poetry.   I. Blue
Mountain Arts (Firm)
PS595.L6T45   1995
811.54080354—dc20   95-36006
                                                         CIP

Blue Mountain Press ®

P.O. Box 4549, Boulder, Colorado 80306

CONTENTS

This Valentine's Day, I Promise You All My Love

I promise to give you all my love
for now and forever,
to keep your love close to my heart
so that we never grow apart.
I promise to confide in you
if I feel insecure.
I promise not to doubt
your judgments or actions,
without first listening
to the feelings in your heart.
I promise to support you in everything
you try to accomplish,
because your goals have become our goals
to achieve together, side by side.
I promise to look back on
the good and bad times with a smile,
to learn by each mistake
and know that, with every step of success,
we will make it if we just try.
I promise to offer you all the happiness
I am capable of giving you,
to see that the future is ours
to make the best of.
I promise to set time aside
to be best friends,
to dream dreams and make them reality,
and just to say "I love you."
I promise most of all
never to take you for granted,
because you are the love of my life.

— Michele Thomas

Sometimes It's Not Enough Just to Say "I Love You"...

Even though I do love you,
I feel I need to express more,
because there is so much more
to our relationship.

Sometimes I need to tell you that
you're the love I live for,
you're my dream made into reality.
Yours are the arms that
hold me close,
and it is your smile that brings
a ray of sunshine
to even the darkest of days.
You are the one who tells me
to keep believing in myself,
in you, and in us.

You have become a part of me
I could never live without,
and as long as I'm living,
as long as you care,
I'll be here for you.
This is a special time in our lives,
because we are sharing it together.

— Janine Stahl

My Love for You Will Never Change

*T*hings come and go in my life;
thoughts and feelings change,
but my love for you always remains,
growing stronger each day.
I love you always.
You've given me some of the nicest times
I've ever known.
You have been, and you are,
my dearest friend and my cherished love.
Most importantly, you are yourself:
the most desirable, exciting person
I have ever known,
filling a place in my life that only you can.
I care for you in ways
I've never known before.
You've given me more than
I'd ever expected to find,
shown me things about myself
I never knew before,
and let me experience the joy
of loving someone who's perfect for me.
I am forever grateful
for each moment we have together,
for the hope and excitement I feel
with each thought of tomorrow and you.
I feel so fortunate to hold your love
in the center of my life and heart.

— Garry LaFollette

I had a huge crush on you right from the start... and I have fallen in love with you more every day... I love your laughing eyes and the way your sensitive spirit shines through... When I'm with you, everything is more magical to me... I cherish our talks, our hugs, our walks, and the way my hand fits so nicely into yours... You're really something wonderful, and I want you to know... that you make me feel loved and happy and filled with very special feelings... Nothing has been the same since you came into my life... but then how could it be... since you made everything a million times better... than I ever imagined it could be.

— Chris Gallatin

I Love You This Much...

Enough to do anything for you —
  give my life, my love, my heart,
  and my soul to you and for you.
Enough to willingly give all of my
  time, efforts, thoughts, talents,
  trust, and prayers to you.
Enough to want to protect you,
  care for you, guide you, hold you,
  comfort you, listen to you, and
  cry to you and with you.
Enough to be completely comfortable
  with you, act silly around you,
  never have to hide anything from
  you, and be myself with you.
Enough to share all of my sentiments,
  dreams, goals, fears, hopes, and
  worries — my entire life with you.
Enough to want the best for you,
  to wish for your successes,
  and to hope for the fulfillment
  of all your endeavors.

*I love you enough to keep my promises
    to you and pledge my loyalty and
    faithfulness to you.*
*Enough to cherish your friendship,
    adore your personality, respect your
        values, and see you for who you are.*
*Enough to fight for you, compromise
    for you, and sacrifice myself for you
    if need be.*
*Enough to miss you incredibly when
    we're apart, no matter what length
    of time it's for and regardless of
    the distance.*
*Enough to believe in our relationship,
    to stand by it through the worst
    of times, to have faith in our
    strength as a couple, and to never
    give up on us.*
*Enough to spend the rest of my life
    with you, be there for you when you
    need or want me, and never, ever want
    to leave you or live without you.*

I love you this much.

— *Lisa M. Thomas*

You Are My World, You Are My Love

What if we had never met?
What would I be doing?
What kind of life would I have?
I often think about these things
and I always come to the same conclusion—
without you
I would be an extremely unhappy person
living an unhappy life

I know that we met for a reason
and that reason was that
you and I were meant to be
in love with each other
You and I were meant to be
a team giving us strength
to function happily in the world
I am so thankful that things
turned out the way they did
and we were brought together
You are my world
You are my love

— Susan Polis Schutz

This Is
Why I Love You

For the kindness in your eyes
   and the warmth in your voice;
for the honesty of your words
   and the silence of your smile;
for the ways in which we're similar
   and those in which we're worlds apart;
for the openness of your understanding
   and the acceptance of your heart;
for the tenderness of your touch
   and the strength of your commitment;
for your sense of humor
   and your seriousness of purpose;
for a thousand small reasons
   and one most important of all —
simply because you are you.

In all of creation,
   you are the one whom I cherish most,
the one with whom I hope
to share my life —
   its joys, its sorrows,
   its accomplishments, its challenges —
while building our dreams together
and growing every day
in the love that makes us one.

— Janet Alampi

You're the Person I Always Dreamed of Loving

I guess you could say that in some ways,
I've always loved you.
That doesn't sound right, I know,
because I haven't always known you.
But I've always known certain qualities
that were important to me,
and in my mind and heart, I've always
carried an image, a fantasy, a wish, I guess,
of a wonderful person I could love totally.
You've given me what I've always wished for:
    fun and laughter,
    concern and understanding,
    a friend to depend on,
    a lover to cherish,
    a partner in everything I do.
I love you so much,
and thinking about you —
how you make me feel,
how I feel about you
and all that you are —
I realize that all my life
I've always loved you in my dreams.
Now that you've come out of my dreams
and into my life,
I can tell you that I've always loved you
and that I always will.

— Garry LaFollette

We Were Made
for One Another

Just as the ocean was made
   to reflect the sunset,
   the stars to answer wishes,
   and dreams to carry hope,
so was our love made
   for a special purpose.

We are a perfect match in love,
   like fire and warmth,
   smiles and laughter.
Both of us are independently strong,
   yet we are made more complete
      through the strength of each other.
Together, we create
   a new blend of beauty and love,
      never before experienced,
      never to be repeated,
      and destined to endure forever.
Some things were just meant to be...
   like you and I.

—Barbara Vecqueray

1 Feel So Lucky
to Have Your Love

Once in a lifetime,
   you find someone
who touches not only your heart,
   but also your soul.
Once in a lifetime,
   you discover someone
who stands beside you, not over you.
   You find someone
who loves you for who you are,
   and not for who you could be.
Once in a lifetime,
   if you're lucky,
you find someone...
   as I have found you.

— Nanci Brillant

The True Meaning of Love

Love doesn't mean that you will never feel pain or live a life free from care. It doesn't mean that you will never be hurt or that your life will be perfect, with every moment consumed by happiness. Love does mean that you will always have a companion, someone to help you through the difficult times and rejoice with you in your times of celebration. Love does mean that each argument is followed by a time of forgiveness, and each time of sorrow is far outweighed by all the tender moments spent in each other's arms.

Love is the miracle that can take two lives and mold them into one, take two souls and bind them for life, take two hearts and fill them with enough passion and tenderness to last a lifetime.

Love is a blessing that will lead you down life's most beautiful path.

— Michele Weber

You Will Always Be the Only Valentine for Me

My mind often drifts back
to the first time we met.
I keep trying to figure out
how this happened to us.
What did we do or say
to bring us so close together
and keep us there all the time?
Maybe there never was meant
to be an explanation;
I don't think I even want one...
One day you just find someone
who touches a secret place
   within you,
and you are never ever the same.

Now, you are making every dream
   of mine come true.
You are the best thing
   that will ever happen to me:
your love, and the way it's lasted,
its constant power and endurance.
No one else will ever
love me like you,
and there is no one else but you
I will ever want.

— Bonna Cook

When a Man and a Woman Are in Love...

His life lies within hers
and her life lies within his.
Each lives as an individual,
    yet they also live
        for one another;
each strives for independent goals,
    but they also work together
        to achieve their goals.

They will give to one another
    what they need to survive
and help fulfill each other's wants.
They will turn
one another's disappointment
    into satisfaction.
They will turn
one another's frustration
    into contentment.

They will work as a mirror,
    reflecting to each other
        their strengths and weaknesses.
They will work together
    to alleviate the emotional walls
        that may separate them.
They will work to build
    a better understanding of one another.

When a man and a woman are in love,
they will learn to lean on each other,
    but not so much as to be
        a burden on the other.
They will learn to reach out to one another,
    but not so much as to suffocate the other.
They will learn when it is time to speak
    and when it is time to listen.

They will be there to comfort each other
    in times of sorrow.
They will be there
    to celebrate with each other
        in times of happiness.
They will be one another's friend,
    guiding each other to the happiness
        that life holds.
They will be one another's companion,
    facing together the challenges
        that life may present.

When a man and a woman are in love,
his life lies within hers
    and her life lies within his.
Together they will love one another
    for the rest of their lives.

— Stephen T. Fader

On Valentine's Day,
I Remember the First Times
I Said... "I Love You"

"*I* love you."
*I remember the first few times
I told you that, and how uncertain I felt,
and how hesitant I was
to let you know how much I really cared.
And yet you smiled, you held me close,
you showed me how true
love was going to be
between us.
From that time on,
and including today,
every time my heart says
"I love you,"
I know how absolutely
wonderful and beautiful
being in love can be
with you.*

— *Deanna Beisser*

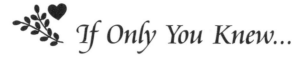 *If Only You Knew...*

*If only you knew how happy
  you have made me,
how important you are to me,
  and how cherished you are
  in my heart...*

If only you knew the warmth
  of your face,
the sparkle in your eyes,
and the radiance of your
  smile...

If only you knew how safe
   I feel when I'm near you,
the lengths I would go
   to make you happy,
and the strength
   of my feelings for you...

If only you knew how lonely
   I am when we're apart,
how lucky I feel to be
   a part of your life,
and how wonderful you truly are...

If only you knew what you
   mean to me,
you would look me in the eyes
   and simply say...
      "I love you, too."

— Matthew Dietzel

All I Want
in the World Is You

Out of anything
   in the world that
   I could hope for,
there is only
   one thing
   that I truly want.

It isn't something
   you can buy;
it's something
   you feel and know.

It's happiness and love;
   it's being able to love
   and knowing you are
   loved in return.

The only thing
   that I really want,
the only thing
   that seems or feels right...

   is you.

—Tia M. Sager

❤❤ Just Remember That I Love You

When it's raining outside
and you're all alone;
when you fall asleep
with a sad face;
when everybody seems
to be against you;
or if you think
that nobody cares,
just remember I love you.

I hope you never forget this.
Because sometimes I also
feel lonely,
and sometimes it rains in my life,
and sometimes I fall asleep
with tears in my eyes.
I have some of those days
when I feel that everybody
is against me
and nobody cares.
Whenever I do, I always remember
that you love me,
and the insecurities
and pain go away.
So please, always remember...
I love you.

— Kristen Marie Lassiter

My Love for You
Is like a Rainbow

Have you ever followed
a rainbow,
only to find it has no end?

That's the way my love is
for you...

My love for you will last
for as long as there is a sky
and as long as the earth stands
beneath my feet.

You are my soulmate,
my purpose for being.
And like a rainbow stretched
across the sky,
my love
for you
has
no
end.

— Jane Maness

A Poem, a Present,
and a Promise
for Valentine's Day

A Poem

*Until you... I never would have believed that
I could feel the happiness I do. Beyond what
any words can say, beyond my wildest dreams
and my sweetest thoughts, you have given me
the happiest days anyone could ask for.
Yesterday I loved you with all my heart.
But today... I love you even more.*

A Present

*If I could, I would give you the moon and the
stars and a million wishes to wish on. But even
though I can't give you everything, I can give
you something. I can give you this reminder:
that you will always have all the gratitude
my heart can hold. I give you my warmest
thanks... for being so wonderful to me.*

And a Promise

*I will try, in everything I do, to live up to the
gift that I have been given: the gift of sharing
so much with you. In all of my days, I promise
that no heart will ever be happier... and no love
will be more true.*

— Carey Martin

The ABC's of
a Good Relationship

*A*lways listen with your heart.
  Hear more than just what is
  being said.
*B*elieve in yourselves. Be
  understanding and accepting.
  No two people are alike; see
  each other's point of view.
*C*ommunicate. (As much as we'd
  like them to be, our partners
  aren't mind readers.) Open up
  and don't be afraid to show your
  true feelings. Create an
  atmosphere where feelings are
  accepted and talked about.
*D*on't judge. Accept the other for
  who they are — the unique individual
  you fell in love with.

*Expect happiness. Have fun. Allow
   humor to get you through some of
   life's stresses.*
*Fear nothing. Trust in each other
   and the love you share. Together,
   you can do anything.*
*Give of yourself: your time, your
   energy, your affection.*
*Help whenever you can by listening,
   caring, and doing.*
*Initiate affection, laughter, fun,
   and play.*
*Just be yourself. Don't ever pretend
   to be what you aren't.*
*Kiss and make up. Don't hold a grudge.
   Forgive and forget.*
*Love unconditionally, patiently,
   passionately, hopefully,
   and enduringly.*

*(If you can do all of these,
   you don't need the rest
   of the alphabet!)*

— Barbara Cage

Our Love Is
the Most Beautiful
Valentine Gift of All

When I am in your arms,
my heart feels so much love.
When I look into your eyes,
I see truth and understanding.
When I hear your voice,
I'm comforted and loved.
I carry your love with me
no matter where I am;
it guides me
and lets me know I am
free to be just me.

You've shown me how to find
what's beautiful in myself;
your love has set me free
to be the best I can be.
You listen when I cry
and you touch me with your hope;
no love is sweeter
than the one we are sharing.
I don't need gifts of candy,
flowers, or balloon bouquets;
your love is the most beautiful gift
you could ever give me.

—Jacqueline Schiff

The One Thing
I'd Never Change in My Life
Is My Love for You

*Life is full of choices.
Its path is lined with many doors —
some that are opening
and others that are closing —
and through each door
is yet another path.*

*Each door is one way.
Once we enter, we can never go back;
we are bound to our past choices.
We can only look back
and wonder "what if"
or perhaps even wish
that we had made different choices.*

*Given the chance,
many people would change directions,
follow another path,
and slip through a different door.*

*I have regrets in my life, too.
But there is one decision,
one choice,
that I would never change:*

>   *being with you.*

— Stephanie L. Sloman

All l ever need is you
to kiss away the tears
and wipe away my frowns.
All l ever need is your love
to help me through lonely nights
and to make me smile
after a long day.
All l ever need is to hear
you whisper softly
   "l love you"
when l wake in the morning
and before l fall asleep at night
   to make my life fully complete.

— Shelly Roberts

LOVE

Love talks, love listens, love
understands ♥ It encourages when in
doubt ♥ It forgives without condition ♥
It has no memory of past offenses ♥
It has a clear-cut set of ideals ♥
It travels a secure path of confidence
and hope ♥ It never examines its
failures or reminds you of your
shortcomings ♥ It looks towards the
future with great anticipation ♥
It knows that when two hearts work
towards one common goal, anything
can be accomplished ♥ Love never
overshadows or domineers ♥ It gives
not only out of a sense of responsibility,
but out of a sense of respect ♥ It
affirms and supports ♥ It uplifts ♥ It
knows how to play, how to laugh, how
to have fun ♥ It knows that to have a
sense of humor is to build a strong and
firm foundation ♥ It doesn't exist for its
own purpose ♥ It lives to share: thought
to thought, soul to soul, spirit to spirit ♥
Love is the gift that continually gives ♥
For where love dwells, happiness
thrives, and never gives up.

— Linda E. Knight

I Love Having You as My Valentine

I love the way we are
when we're together,
the times we make into
    our very own,
the fun you put
    into everything,
the happiness that
    you give me.

I love being with you,
    seeing you,
        and touching you.
I love just knowing
that you are there.
I love getting lost
in my thoughts of you.

I love what my life is with you,
though I can't always put
my feelings into words.
I love the times when,
for so many different reasons,
everything is just so right between us.
All that matters to me,
every dream I ever dared to have,
is here for me in the love we share.

I love the way I feel about you.
I love the way I love you.
I love having you as my valentine!

— *Garry LaFollette*

Some people believe
that with time
relationships become
less interesting
less exciting and
less fun
But our relationship
with time
has become more interesting
more exciting and
more fun
Some people believe
that with time
the best aspects of a relationship end
But with time
our relationship
has gotten better and better
and our love has become
stronger and stronger
Our relationship is the
most important
part of my life and
I will always strive
to keep it this way

I believe so much in
you and in us and
I love you so much

— Susan Polis Schutz

Sometimes I Wonder If You Know How Much I Love You

Sometimes when you look at me,
I wonder if you see all the love
that shines in my eyes only for you.
I wonder if you see in my smile
the special touch of happiness
that comes from loving you.
When you look into my eyes,
I feel you reaching deep within my soul,
and I wonder if you see
all the beautiful light in me
that comes from your love.
I wonder if you see
my arms reaching out to hold you
with tenderness and warmth.
I wonder if you see
the fullness of my heart
and the precious feelings our love brings.

Sometimes I want to tell you
to look with your heart,
and you'll see that
everything I have to give
is only for you, for always.

— Linda Sackett-Morrison

You Are My
One True Valentine

The days we share are my blessings.
The memories we make are
     my treasures.
The togetherness we have is
     my dream come true.
And the understanding we share is
     something I've never had
          with anyone but you.

If anyone ever asked me
what part of my life you are...
          I would just have to
          look at them and smile
and say, "The BEST part."

The happiness you give to me
is something I'll never
     be able to get enough of.

I love having you in my world.

     And I love having you to love.

— Chris Gallatin

I Belong in Your Arms

Finally
I have found a place
Into which
I fit
  Perfectly,
  Safely,
  And securely,
    With no doubts,
    No fears,
    No sadness,
    No tears.

This place is filled
  With happiness
And laughter,
Yet it is spacious enough
To allow me
The freedom to move around,
  To live my life
  And be myself.
This wonderful place,
Which I never believed really existed,
I have found
Finally
  Inside your arms,
  Inside your heart,
  Inside your love.

— Deborah A. Brideau

You Are All
I Ever Wanted

I always wanted someone special in my life.
I wanted someone who cared about me
and understood my feelings;
someone who would listen to my worries
and try to help me ease my way through them.
I wanted someone who would be patient with me
when I needed a little more time and tolerance;
someone who didn't expect or demand
that I try to be someone I'm not,
and who wouldn't try to manipulate me
into their idea of a perfect mate.
I wanted someone who knew how to give —
not just on special occasions
or when it's easy or convenient,
but every day —
whenever there was a moment
that we could share.

I wanted someone who would make time for me
regardless of busy and hectic schedules;
I wanted to know that I mattered
and that I was more important
than a business deal.
I wanted someone in my life who knew
what love and loving mean
and who allowed themselves every opportunity
to enjoy those wonderful feelings.
I wanted someone who had hopes and dreams
about happiness and the future, just as I did.

As you probably know by now...
you are the person who fits all my ideals.
When it comes to the special someone in my life,
you are all I ever wanted.

— *Deanna Beisser*

If not for you,
I wonder where I would be right now
and what road in life
I would have taken.
There were so many directions
I could have chosen,
but none of them would have
been more fulfilling.

For me, fulfillment is
knowing that I am sharing my life
with someone who is not only
beautiful outside, but inside, too;
someone whose true character
is revealed through your kindness
and understanding.

It gives me a very special feeling
to know that I'm sharing my life
with someone who is not just
the love of my life,
but also the greatest friend
a person could ever have.

— Austin Hamblin

I Promise
That I Will Love You

I cannot promise you that
I will not change
I cannot promise you that
I will not have many different moods
I cannot promise you that
I will not hurt your feelings sometimes
I cannot promise you that
I will not be erratic
I cannot promise you that
I will always be strong
I cannot promise you that
my faults will not show

But —
I do promise you that
I will always be supportive of you
I do promise you that
I will share all my thoughts
*   and feelings with you*
I do promise you that
I will give you freedom to be yourself
I do promise you that
I will understand everything that you do
I do promise you that
I will be completely honest with you
I do promise you that
I will laugh and cry with you
I do promise you that
I will help you achieve all your goals
But —
most of all
I do promise you that
I will love you

— Susan Polis Schutz

Thank You for Loving Me

Thank you for each moment
  spent together,
  each thought and word shared.
Thank you for being honest,
  even when it would have
  been easier not to be.
Thank you for each tear
  you've turned to laughter,
  for each heartache
  you've turned to joy.
Thank you for making me
  feel beautiful inside and out.
Thank you for lifting me beyond
  my insecurities with your words
  of confidence and praise.
Thank you for accepting me
  as I am and for overlooking
  the faults I know I have.
Thank you for being the person
  that you are, and for helping me
  to be the person I have become.
Thank you for loving me,
  as I love you.

— Deanne Laura Gilbert

On Valentine's Day,
When I Say "I Love You"...

I say the words "I love you" so much
that I wonder sometimes if you take for
granted the feeling that is behind them.
I never want you to see them as just words
to begin or end a conversation.
"I love you" is just my way of saying
that you have touched a place in my
heart and made me come alive.

You have claimed a part of my heart
that, no matter what happens to us,
will always belong to you.
You taught me how to love.
You broke through all of my defenses
and comforted my fears.

You touched places in me
*   I never knew I had,*
and made me feel things
*   I never thought I'd feel.*
You have all of the patience, care,
understanding, and concern needed
to build the kind of relationship we have.

So when I say "I love you,"
the words are not spoken out of habit.
It is my way of saying thank you for
being you and of returning some
of the joy you have given me.

— *Arletha Miles*

ACKNOWLEDGMENTS

The following is a partial list of authors whom the publisher especially wishes to thank for permission to reprint their works.

Michele Weber for "The True Meaning of Love." Copyright © 1995 by Michele Weber. All rights reserved. Reprinted by permission.

Stephen T. Fader for "When a Man and a Woman Are in Love...." Copyright © 1995 by Stephen T. Fader. All rights reserved. Reprinted by permission.

Kristen Marie Lassiter for "Just Remember That I Love You." Copyright © 1995 by Kristen Marie Lassiter. All rights reserved. Reprinted by permission.

Jane Maness for "My Love for You Is like a Rainbow." Copyright © 1995 by Jane Maness. All rights reserved. Reprinted by permission.

Barbara Cage for "The ABC's of a Good Relationship." Copyright © 1995 by Barbara Cage. All rights reserved. Reprinted by permission.

Jacqueline Schiff for "Our Love Is the Most Beautiful Valentine Gift of All." Copyright © 1995 by Jacqueline Schiff. All rights reserved. Reprinted by permission.

Stephanie L. Sloman for "The One Thing I'd Never Change...." Copyright © 1995 by Stephanie L. Sloman. All rights reserved. Reprinted by permission.

Linda E. Knight for "LOVE." Copyright © 1995 by Linda E. Knight. All rights reserved. Reprinted by permission.

A careful effort has been made to trace the ownership of poems used in this anthology in order to obtain permission to reprint copyrighted materials and give proper credit to the copyright owners. If any error or omission has occurred, it is completely inadvertent, and we would like to make corrections in future editions provided that written notification is made to the publisher: BLUE MOUNTAIN PRESS, INC., P.O. Box 4549, Boulder, Colorado 80306.

If you are interested in submitting your original poetry to Blue Mountain Press for possible inclusion in a future anthology, please write for guidelines or send your work with SASE to: BMA Editorial Department, P. O. Box 1007, Dept. BP, Boulder, Colorado 80306.